Inflation and How to make wealth during a high inflation period.

Table of contents

Chapter one

Today's inflation is being fuelled in part by supply issues, but boosting productivity would help tackle this.
Producing more goods and services in a shorter time would cut costs per unit and raise supply, putting downward pressure on prices.
Governments need to incentivise investment to achieve this, by cutting taxes and developing strategic plans for different regions.
Inflation has become one of the great issues of our times. The UK's is the highest in the G7, weighing in at 9% a year according to the most recent figures on consumer price inflation.

When you look at the other common measure for prices, retail price inflation, which adds mortgage rates into the equation and is also calculated a little differently, it is even higher at 11%. This is important because RPI is used for raising prices across a range of items, from train tickets and mobile phone contracts to student loans.

The question of why inflation is so high is well rehearsed. The initial impetus came from greater demand, but it is being further fuelled by supply issues.

What caused high inflation
On the demand side, quantitative easing (QE) during the pandemic – in which central banks "created money" to help prop up the economy – has increased the amount of money in the system by over 20%.

When lockdown ended, this helped to ensure that there was pent-up demand for goods and services: retail sales rose by over 20% year on year in May 2021, for instance, and hit another peak of nearly 10% in January 2022. At the same time, demand from firms helped to drive huge price increases in key industrial commodities such as copper and steel. Also, oil prices rose by approximately 67% in 2021 and another 20% in 2022 to date.

Heightened demand has collided with constraints on the global supply chain from social distancing, self-isolation rules and renewed lockdowns in China (even the Ever Given getting stuck). As a result, the cost of shipping goods is around 35% higher than the pre-pandemic high (and over 700% higher than its low). And all of this is before discussing the war in Ukraine.

The response by the Bank of England has been to increase the headline rate of interest from 0.1% to 1%, and to stop QE. Tightening monetary policy affects demand as the interest due on many debt repayments is rising and the cost of borrowing is going up. As a result, the GfK UK consumer confidence index is sitting at -40, a historically low level (when the number is positive, it means consumer confidence is high).

This combination of higher interest rates and higher prices has increased the likelihood of a recession. In part, this is because increasing interest rates discourages businesses from investing. But there's also another problem with discouraging investment: it's part of the long-term solution to our inflation problem.

Productivity and investment
This is linked to the UK's long-term problem with productivity: in other words, how much each worker produces. The UK productivity rate is growing, which you would expect as technology brings improvements, but the growth is less than that of key international competitors like the US, Germany and France.

While the rate of growth has returned to pre-pandemic levels after plunging during the lockdowns, it is still slower than in the years before the global financial crisis of 2007-09. A PwC report from 2019 highlights that annual growth in UK productivity was 2% for the ten years to 2008 and 0.6% for the ten years after, with a productivity gap of approximately 10% to Germany and over 30% to the US.

.

Construction workers digging up a road
Boosting productivity could help tackle high inflation rates. Image: Unsplash/Mika Baumeister.

Today's inflation is being fuelled in part by supply issues, but boosting productivity would help tackle this.
Producing more goods and services in a shorter time would cut costs per unit and raise supply, putting downward pressure on prices.

Governments need to incentivise investment to achieve this, by cutting taxes and developing strategic plans for different regions.

Inflation has become one of the great issues of our times. The UK's is the highest in the G7, weighing in at 9% a year according to the most recent figures on consumer price inflation.

When you look at the other common measure for prices, retail price inflation, which adds mortgage rates into the equation and is also calculated a little differently, it is even higher at 11%. This is important because RPI is used for raising prices across a range of items, from train tickets and mobile phone contracts to student loans.

The question of why inflation is so high is well rehearsed. The initial impetus came from greater demand, but it is being further fuelled by supply issues.

Chapter two

What caused high inflation:
On the demand side, quantitative easing (QE) during the pandemic – in which central banks "created money" to help prop up the economy – has increased the amount of money in the system by over 20%.

When lockdown ended, this helped to ensure that there was pent-up demand for goods and services: retail sales rose by over 20% year on year in May 2021, for instance, and hit another peak of nearly 10% in January 2022. At the same time, demand from firms helped to drive huge price increases in key industrial commodities such as copper and steel. Also, oil prices rose by approximately 67% in 2021 and another 20% in 2022 to date.

Heightened demand has collided with constraints on the global supply chain from social distancing, self-isolation rules and renewed lockdowns in China (even the Ever Given getting stuck). As a result, the cost of shipping goods is around 35% higher than the pre-pandemic high (and over 700% higher than its low). And all of this is before discussing the war in Ukraine.

The response by the Bank of England has been to increase the headline rate of interest from 0.1% to 1%, and to stop QE. Tightening monetary policy affects demand as the interest due on many debt repayments is rising and the cost of borrowing is going up. As a result, the GfK UK consumer confidence index is sitting at -40, a historically low level (when the number is positive, it means consumer confidence is high).

This combination of higher interest rates and higher prices has increased the likelihood of a recession. In part, this is because increasing interest rates discourages businesses from investing. But there's also another problem with discouraging investment: it's part of the long-term solution to our inflation problem.

Productivity and investment
This is linked to the UK's long-term problem with productivity: in other words, how much each worker produces. The UK productivity rate is growing, which you would expect as technology brings improvements, but the growth is less than that of key international competitors like the US, Germany and France.

While the rate of growth has returned to pre-pandemic levels after plunging during the lockdowns, it is still slower than in the years before the global financial crisis of 2007-09. A PwC report from 2019 highlights that annual growth in UK productivity was 2% for the ten years to 2008 and 0.6% for the ten years after, with a productivity gap of approximately 10% to Germany and over 30% to the US.

G7 productivity growth, 1997-2021

A chart showing G7 productivity growth, 1997-2021
Growth over time seems to be following an upward trend in US Image: The Conversation/ONS

Why does productivity matter for inflation? When a workforce is more productive it produces more goods and services, and at a lower cost per unit. This means there is a greater supply of these things, which puts downward pressure on prices and is therefore associated with lower inflation.

How do we raise productivity? One important way is to invest more, but this has been a weakness in the UK. Business investment plateaued in 2016 following the Brexit referendum, fell with COVID-19 and remains almost 10% below the 2019 level. The nation's investment spending as a proportion of GDP (16.7%) compares poorly with the US (22.5%), Japan (25%) and the EU (24.3%). This is despite evidence that UK companies are holding £140 billion in cash and have a backlog of accumulated projects.

What can be done:
The question is how to encourage firms to release this investment potential. The government is planning to increase headline corporation tax from 19% to 25% in 2023, which is not going to help and should arguably be scrapped. To further incentivise investment, there's also a need for more generous rules around tax relief, including extending the "super-deduction" that was brought in two years ago, which can reduce companies' tax bills by 25%. As well as encouraging companies to invest and expand, the government needs to incentivise people to start new companies. For example, the UK has lost three-quarters of a million self-employed workers since February 2020.

To encourage more start-ups, the UK government, the devolved administrations and councils need to come together to develop strategic plans for different regions. This includes making better use of universities as local hubs for expertise and developing clusters of similar firms based on local specialisms that can help one another by sharing equipment and collaborating. Plans exist, but need to be actioned; levelling up must be more than a catchy slogan.

Public investment has to be part of the picture. This especially includes education, both at school, where upgraded facilities are required to ensure that young people are fully trained in the latest technology; and for over-18s, with a clearer balance between university and apprenticeship training.

Getting east to west is about to become substantially easier in London thanks to Crossrail, but remains tortuous elsewhere, whether from Leeds to Manchester or Edinburgh Glasgow. Quicker transport links improve the mobility of goods and labour, while truly upgrading internet connections (full fibre and 5G) improves links when travel isn't necessary. Both improve productivity. Inevitably, these kinds of interventions involve further spending. But this has to be viewed as a long-term solution. After WWII, government debt was well over 200% of GDP and took 50 years to be paid off. The same time scale can be considered now.

UK Chancellor Rishi Sunak has been talking a lot about the need to unlock investment and raise productivity, but there is still very little detail about what the government intends to do. There are lots of economic benefits to raising productivity, but bringing down inflation is the one that everyone seems to have missed.

Chapter Three

Timeless Ways to Protect Yourself From Inflation.
In addition to death and taxes, inflation is another phenomenon that we can expect with near certainty over a period of time.

The U.S. has actually gone through many brief periods of deflation, but in general, economic progress is accompanied by inflationary pressures. Inflation may occur when there is too much money in the system, which leads to an escalation in the price of goods. Of course, if a household's two primary sources of wealth creation—asset and income appreciation—rise at a rate equal to or greater than inflation, the negative effects of inflation are neutralised.

Yet, as we've seen time and again, that usually is not the case. While the minimum wage has increased, the overall price of goods has outpaced the average salary increases of recent years.

Economic Policy Institute. "Raising the Federal Minimum Wage to $15 By 2024 Would Lift Pay for Nearly 40 Million Workers."
The Worst Tax

Inflation is often referred to as the "worst tax" because its effects go unnoticed by most people. Hypothetically, earning 4% in a savings account while inflation grows at 7% makes many feel 4% richer. In fact, they are 3% poorer.
That's why it's important for households and investors alike to understand the causes and effects of inflation, and how to plan so as to ensure that their assets maintain their purchasing power.

Here are three investment approaches everyone should consider as ways of protecting their hard-earned wealth from the ravages of inflation.

Invest in Stocks:
Despite the lack of confidence most people express about stocks, owning some equities can be a very good way to combat inflation. Think of your household as a business. If a company cannot properly invest its money in projects that will deliver a return above its costs, then it, too, will fall victim to inflation. The basic premise of business success is that corporations will sell their goods at increasing prices, which will lead to elevated revenues, earnings, and inevitably, stock prices. Some of the best stocks to own during inflation would be in companies that can increase their prices naturally during inflationary periods.

Commodity resource companies are one example. Products like oil, grains, and metals enjoy pricing power during periods of inflation. The prices of these items tend to go up as opposed to, for example, the price of a computer, which is subject to manufacturer and distributor price adjustments.
Still, price increases aren't enough to protect against inflation. If a company experiences rising expenses, price increases alone are not enough to maintain equity appreciation. That's why grocery stores, which may benefit from an increase in food prices, may also suffer from an increase in their cost of goods sold.

Look to invest in businesses such as commodity firms or healthcare companies that possess the strongest profit margins and, generally, the lowest cost of production. Finally, never underestimate the value of dividends during periods of inflation. Dividends increase the total return of a portfolio.

Invest in a Home:

When done for the right reasons, like buying a home to live in, real estate is always a good investment. Problems occur when a buyer's goal is to flip the property they just bought at a profit. Although experienced real estate investors are able to find hidden values in properties, the average person should focus on purchasing a home with the intent of holding it, even if only for a few years. Real estate investments do not typically generate a return within several months or weeks; they require an extensive waiting period in order for values to increase.

As a home buyer, unless you're paying cash, you're likely to put some money down and take out a loan, known as a mortgage, for the remainder of the purchase price. There are different types of mortgages—fixed-rate and adjustable are the most common—but the underlying principle is the same. You pay off a little of the principal each month until you're left with ownership of a debt-free asset that should continue to appreciate over time.

If you get a fixed-rate mortgage, you end up paying off future debt with cheaper currency if rates increase. But if rates decrease, you're still responsible for the fixed amount. Various factors should be taken into account in order to determine your best mortgage option.

Like land, home prices tend to increase in value on an average year-over-year basis. It is true that real estate bubbles are usually followed by correctional periods, sometimes causing homes to lose over half of their value. Still, on average, housing prices tend to increase over time, counteracting the effects of inflation.

Invest in Yourself:
By far the best investment you can make to be prepared for an uncertain financial future is an investment in yourself. One that will increase your future earning power.

This investment begins with quality education and continues with keeping skills up-to-date and learning new skills that will match those most needed in the not-too-distant future. Being able to stay on top of a business's changing needs may not only help to inflation-proof your salary, but also recession-proof your career.

Chapter four

10 Common Effects of Inflation

Inflation is the overall rise in the prices of goods and services over time. The annual inflation rate in the United States averaged 3.27% between 1914 and 2022.

1

As such, moderate inflation has been a fact of life and the natural economic state for more than a century.

This makes it important to distinguish between the inherent effects of inflation at any rate and those that only come into play during periods when inflation runs unusually high. We'll do that below by identifying inflation's most important effects on consumers, investors, and the economy.

KEY TAKEAWAYS
- Inflation is the sustained and broad rise in the prices of goods and services over time, which erodes purchasing power.
- Inflation is generally caused by an imbalance in supply and demand, supply shocks, and inflation expectations.
- A small but positive inflation rate is economically useful, while high inflation tends to feed on itself and impair the economy's long-term performance.
- Real estate, energy commodities, and value stocks have historically outperformed during periods of high or rising inflation.
- Bonds and expensive growth stocks tend to lag as inflation lowers the present value of their future cash flows to investors.

What Causes Inflation?

Inflation is the rise in prices of goods and services over a certain period of time. When prices rise, consumers lose purchasing power, which means the power of a single unit of currency doesn't go as far as it did before. A little inflation isn't much cause for concern but it can be when prices rise too quickly. But what causes this increase?

Some of the most common factors that lead to inflation include:

- An imbalance in supply and demand. Inflation tends to increase when consumer demand for goods and services increases when supplies are limited at desirable price levels.
- The disruption in supplies or supply shocks can trigger inflation. For instance, global energy prices jumped following Russia's invasion of Ukraine. Russia cut off global energy supplies and tightened the market in response to sanctions placed by the international community. This drop in energy supplies caused prices to increase.
- The expectations of inflation. When people expect prices to rise, they often demand higher wages in order to prepare for future price increases. Producers and businesses tend to respond by raising prices, which causes inflation to rise.

Now let's take a look at some of the major impacts inflation has on the economy.

1. Inflation Erodes Purchasing Power
This is inflation's primary and most pervasive effect. An overall rise in prices over time reduces the purchasing power of consumers since a fixed amount of money will afford progressively less consumption.

Consumers lose purchasing power regardless of what the inflation rate is—whether it's 2% or 4%. This just means that they lose it twice as fast at the higher rate. Compounding ensures that the overall price level increases more than twice as much over the long run if long-run inflation were to double.

Inflation measures the rise in prices over time for a basket of goods and services representative of overall consumer spending. The Consumer Price Index (CPI) is the best-known inflation indicator, while the Federal Reserve focuses on the PCE Price Index in its inflation targeting.

2. Inflation Disproportionately Impacts Lower-Income Consumers
Lower-income consumers tend to spend a higher proportion of their income on necessities than those with higher incomes. This means they have less of a cushion against the loss of purchasing power inherent in inflation.

Policymakers and financial market participants often focus on core inflation. This measurement of inflation excludes the prices of food and energy because they tend to be more volatile and less reflective of the longer-term inflation trends. But earners with lower income spend a relatively large proportion of their weekly or monthly household budgets on food and energy—commodities that are hard to substitute or go without when prices spike.
The poor are also less likely to own assets like real estate, which has traditionally served as an inflation hedge.

On the other hand, recipients of Social Security benefits and other federal transfer payments receive inflation protection in the form of cost of living adjustments (COLA) based on the Consumer Price Index for Urban Wage Earners and Clerical Workers (CPI-W), which is an index of consumer prices for hourly wage earners and clerical workers.

3.27% between 1914 and 2022.
As such, moderate inflation has been a fact of life and the natural economic state for more than a century.

This makes it important to distinguish between the inherent effects of inflation at any rate and those that only come into play during periods when inflation runs unusually high. We'll do that below by identifying inflation's most important effects on consumers, investors, and the economy.

KEY TAKEAWAYS
Inflation is the sustained and broad rise in the prices of goods and services over time, which erodes purchasing power.
Inflation is generally caused by an imbalance in supply and demand, supply shocks, and inflation expectations.
A small but positive inflation rate is economically useful, while high inflation tends to feed on itself and impair the economy's long-term performance.
Real estate, energy commodities, and value stocks have historically outperformed during periods of high or rising inflation.
Bonds and expensive growth stocks tend to lag as inflation lowers the present value of their future cash flows to investors.
How Can Inflation Be Good For The Economy?

Chapter five

What Causes Inflation?
Inflation is the rise in prices of goods and services over a certain period of time.
When prices rise, consumers lose purchasing power, which means the power of
a single unit of currency doesn't go as far as it did before. A little inflation isn't
much cause for concern but it can be when prices rise too quickly. But what
causes this increase?

Some of the most common factors that lead to inflation include:

An imbalance in supply and demand. Inflation tends to increase when consumer
demand for goods and services increases when supplies are limited at desirable
price levels.
The disruption in supplies or supply shocks can trigger inflation. For instance,
global energy prices jumped following Russia's invasion of Ukraine. Russia cut
off global energy supplies and tightened the market in response to sanctions
placed by the international community. This drop in energy supplies caused
prices to increase.
The expectations of inflation. When people expect prices to rise, they often
demand higher wages in order to prepare for future price increases. Producers
and businesses tend to respond by raising prices, which causes inflation to rise.

Now let's take a look at some of the major impacts inflation has on the
economy.
1. Inflation Erodes Purchasing Power
This is inflation's primary and most pervasive effect. An overall rise in prices
over time reduces the purchasing power of consumers since a fixed amount of
money will afford progressively less consumption.

Consumers lose purchasing power regardless of what the inflation rate
is—whether it's 2% or 4%. This just means that they lose it twice as fast at the
higher rate. Compounding ensures that the overall price level increases more
than twice as much over the long run if long-run inflation were to double.

Inflation measures the rise in prices over time for a basket of goods and services
representative of overall consumer spending. The Consumer Price Index (CPI)

is the best-known inflation indicator, while the Federal Reserve focuses on the PCE Price Index in its inflation targeting.

2. Inflation Disproportionately Impacts Lower-Income Consumers
Lower-income consumers tend to spend a higher proportion of their income on necessities than those with higher incomes. This means they have less of a cushion against the loss of purchasing power inherent in inflation.

Policymakers and financial market participants often focus on core inflation. This measurement of inflation excludes the prices of food and energy because they tend to be more volatile and less reflective of the longer-term inflation trends. But earners with lower income spend a relatively large proportion of their weekly or monthly household budgets on food and energy—commodities that are hard to substitute or go without when prices spike.

The poor are also less likely to own assets like real estate, which has traditionally served as an inflation hedge.

On the other hand, recipients of Social Security benefits and other federal transfer payments receive inflation protection in the form of cost of living adjustments (COLA) based on the Consumer Price Index for Urban Wage Earners and Clerical Workers (CPI-W), which is an index of consumer prices for hourly wage earners and clerical workers.

3. Inflation Keeps Deflation at Bay
The Fed's target inflation rate is set at 2% over the long run. This allows it to meet its mandates for stable prices and maximum employment. It focuses on modest inflation rather than steady prices because a slightly positive inflation rate greases the wheels of commerce, provides a margin of error in the event inflation is overestimated, and deters deflation. The overall decline in prices can be much more destabilising than comparable inflation.

Lenders can charge interest to offset the inflation likely to devalue repayments. It also helps borrowers service their debts by allowing them to make future repayments with inflated currency. On the other hand, deflation makes it more expensive to service debt in real terms, since incomes would be likely to decline alongside prices.

One reason modest inflation (rather than deflation) is the norm is that wages are sticky to the downside. Workers tend to resist attempts to cut their wages during an economic downturn, with layoffs the likeliest alternative for businesses facing a downturn in demand.

A positive inflation rate allows a wage freeze to serve as a cut in labour costs in real terms.

The benefits of inflation are only insurance against deflation until price hikes exceed the customary and expected rate because inflation can also spiral out of control if high enough.

4. Inflation Feeds on Itself When It's High

A little inflation can signal a healthy economy. As such, it's not something that's likely to cause inflation expectations to rise. If inflation was 2% last year and is 2% this year, it's mostly background noise. Businesses, workers, and consumers would likely expect inflation to remain at 2% next year in that scenario.

But expectations of future inflation will begin to rise accordingly when the inflation rate accelerates sharply and stays high. As those expectations rise, workers start demanding larger wage increases and employers pass those costs on by raising prices on output, setting off a wage-price spiral.

In the worst-case scenario, a bungled policy response to high inflation can end in hyperinflation. But there's no need to count the cost of soaring inflation expectations in wheelbarrow loads of Zimbabwe dollar notes denominated in trillions or in the Weimar Republic's worthless marks from Germany's five years of hyperinflation after World War I. In the U.S., rising inflation expectations during the 1970s lifted annual inflation above 13% by 1980 and the federal funds rate to more than 20% by 1981, while unemployment topped 10% as late as mid-1983 following the ensuing recessions.

5. Inflation Raises Interest Rates

As the examples above suggest, governments and central banks have a powerful incentive to keep inflation in check. The approach has been to manage inflation using monetary policy over the past century. When inflation threatens to exceed a central bank's target (typically 2% in developed economies and 3% to 4% in emerging ones), policymakers can raise the minimum interest rate, driving borrowing costs higher across the economy by constraining the money supply.

As a result, inflation and interest rates tend to move in the same direction. By raising interest rates as inflation rises, central banks can dampen the economy's animal spirits or risk appetite, and the attendant price pressures. The expected monthly payments on that boat or that corporate bond issue for a new expansion project suddenly seem a bit high. Meanwhile, the risk-free rate of return available for newly issued Treasury bonds will tend to rise, rewarding savings.

6. Inflation Lowers Debt Service Costs
While new borrowers are likely to face higher interest rates when inflation rises, those with fixed-rate mortgages and other loans get the benefit of repaying these with inflated money, lowering their debt service costs after adjusting for inflation.Say you borrow $1,000 at a 5% annual rate of interest. If annual inflation subsequently rises to 10%, the annual decline in your inflation-adjusted loan balance will outweigh your interest costs.

Note that this doesn't apply to adjustable-rate mortgages (ARMs), credit card balances, or home equity lines of credit (HELOCs), which typically allow lenders to raise their interest rates to keep pace with inflation and Fed rate hikes.

 As such, moderate inflation has been a fact of life and the natural economic state for more than a century.

This makes it important to distinguish between the inherent effects of inflation at any rate and those that only come into play during periods when inflation runs unusually high. We'll do that below by identifying inflation's most important effects on consumers, investors, and the economy.

KEY TAKEAWAYS
Inflation is the sustained and broad rise in the prices of goods and services over time, which erodes purchasing power.
Inflation is generally caused by an imbalance in supply and demand, supply shocks, and inflation expectations.
A small but positive inflation rate is economically useful, while high inflation tends to feed on itself and impair the economy's long-term performance.
Real estate, energy commodities, and value stocks have historically outperformed during periods of high or rising inflation.

Bonds and expensive growth stocks tend to lag as inflation lowers the present value of their future cash flows to investors.
How Can Inflation Be Good For The Economy?

What Causes Inflation?
Inflation is the rise in prices of goods and services over a certain period of time. When prices rise, consumers lose purchasing power, which means the power of a single unit of currency doesn't go as far as it did before. A little inflation isn't much cause for concern but it can be when prices rise too quickly. But what causes this increase?

Chapter six

Some of the most common factors that lead to inflation include:
An imbalance in supply and demand. Inflation tends to increase when consumer demand for goods and services increases when supplies are limited at desirable price levels.
The disruption in supplies or supply shocks can trigger inflation. For instance, global energy prices jumped following Russia's invasion of Ukraine. Russia cut off global energy supplies and tightened the market in response to sanctions placed by the international community. This drop in energy supplies caused prices to increase.
The expectations of inflation. When people expect prices to rise, they often demand higher wages in order to prepare for future price increases. Producers and businesses tend to respond by raising prices, which causes inflation to rise.

Now let's take a look at some of the major impacts inflation has on the economy;

1. Inflation Erodes Purchasing Power
This is inflation's primary and most pervasive effect. An overall rise in prices over time reduces the purchasing power of consumers since a fixed amount of money will afford progressively less consumption.

Consumers lose purchasing power regardless of what the inflation rate is—whether it's 2% or 4%. This just means that they lose it twice as fast at the higher rate. Compounding ensures that the overall price level increases more than twice as much over the long run if long-run inflation were to double.

Inflation measures the rise in prices over time for a basket of goods and services representative of overall consumer spending. The Consumer Price Index (CPI) is the best-known inflation indicator, while the Federal Reserve focuses on the PCE Price Index in its inflation targeting.

2. Inflation Disproportionately Impacts Lower-Income Consumers
Lower-income consumers tend to spend a higher proportion of their income on necessities than those with higher incomes. This means they have less of a cushion against the loss of purchasing power inherent in inflation.

Policymakers and financial market participants often focus on core inflation. This measurement of inflation excludes the prices of food and energy because they tend to be more volatile and less reflective of the longer-term inflation trends. But earners with lower income spend a relatively large proportion of their weekly or monthly household budgets on food and energy—commodities that are hard to substitute or go without when prices spike.

The poor are also less likely to own assets like real estate, which has traditionally served as an inflation hedge.

On the other hand, recipients of Social Security benefits and other federal transfer payments receive inflation protection in the form of cost of living adjustments (COLA) based on the Consumer Price Index for Urban Wage Earners and Clerical Workers (CPI-W), which is an index of consumer prices for hourly wage earners and clerical workers.

3. Inflation Keeps Deflation at Bay
The Fed's target inflation rate is set at 2% over the long run. This allows it to meet its mandates for stable prices and maximum employment. It focuses on modest inflation rather than steady prices because a slightly positive inflation rate greases the wheels of commerce, provides a margin of error in the event inflation is overestimated, and deters deflation. The overall decline in prices can be much more destabilising than comparable inflation.
4

Lenders can charge interest to offset the inflation likely to devalue repayments. It also helps borrowers service their debts by allowing them to make future repayments with inflated currency. On the other hand, deflation makes it more expensive to service debt in real terms, since incomes would be likely to decline alongside prices.

One reason modest inflation (rather than deflation) is the norm is that wages are sticky to the downside. Workers tend to resist attempts to cut their wages during an economic downturn, with layoffs the likeliest alternative for businesses facing a downturn in demand.
5
 A positive inflation rate allows a wage freeze to serve as a cut in labour costs in real terms.

The benefits of inflation are only insurance against deflation until price hikes exceed the customary and expected rate because inflation can also spiral out of control if high enough.

 Because deflation represents a departure from the norm, it's also more likely to trigger expectations for additional deflation, causing further spending and income declines and ultimately widespread loan defaults that can set off a banking crisis.
4. Inflation Feeds on Itself When It's High
A little inflation can signal a healthy economy. As such, it's not something that's likely to cause inflation expectations to rise. If inflation was 2% last year and is 2% this year, it's mostly background noise. Businesses, workers, and consumers would likely expect inflation to remain at 2% next year in that scenario.

But expectations of future inflation will begin to rise accordingly when the inflation rate accelerates sharply and stays high. As those expectations rise, workers start demanding larger wage increases and employers pass those costs on by raising prices on output, setting off a wage-price spiral.

In the worst-case scenario, a bungled policy response to high inflation can end in hyperinflation. But there's no need to count the cost of soaring inflation expectations in wheelbarrow loads of Zimbabwe dollar notes denominated in trillions or in the Weimar Republic's worthless marks from Germany's five years of hyperinflation after World War I. In the U.S., rising inflation expectations during the 1970s lifted annual inflation above 13% by 1980 and the federal funds rate to more than 20% by 1981, while unemployment topped 10% as late as mid-1983 following the ensuing recessions.

Inflation in Weimar Germany
By December 1923, an index of the cost of living in Germany increased to a level of more than 1.5 trillion times its pre-WWI measure.

5. Inflation Raises Interest Rates
As the examples above suggest, governments and central banks have a powerful incentive to keep inflation in check. The approach has been to manage inflation using monetary policy over the past century. When inflation threatens to exceed a central bank's target (typically 2% in developed economies and 3% to 4% in emerging ones), policymakers can raise the minimum interest rate, driving borrowing costs higher across the economy by constraining the money supply.
10
As a result, inflation and interest rates tend to move in the same direction. By raising interest rates as inflation rises, central banks can dampen the economy's animal spirits or risk appetite, and the attendant price pressures. The expected monthly payments on that boat or that corporate bond issue for a new expansion project suddenly seem a bit high. Meanwhile, the risk-free rate of return available for newly issued Treasury bonds will tend to rise, rewarding savings.

6. Inflation Lowers Debt Service Costs
While new borrowers are likely to face higher interest rates when inflation rises, those with fixed-rate mortgages and other loans get the benefit of repaying these with inflated money, lowering their debt service costs after adjusting for inflation.

Say you borrow $1,000 at a 5% annual rate of interest. If annual inflation subsequently rises to 10%, the annual decline in your inflation-adjusted loan balance will outweigh your interest costs.

Note that this doesn't apply to adjustable-rate mortgages (ARMs), credit card balances, or home equity lines of credit (HELOCs), which typically allow lenders to raise their interest rates to keep pace with inflation and Fed rate hikes.

7. Inflation Lifts Growth & Employment in the Short Term

Higher inflation can lead to faster economic growth in the short term. While the 1970s are recalled as a decade of stagflation, U.S. real gross domestic product (GDP) increased 3.2% annually on average between 1970 and 1979, well above the economy's average growth rate since.

Elevated inflation discourages saving since it erodes the purchasing power of the savings over time. That prospect can encourage consumers to spend and businesses to invest.

As a result, unemployment often declines at first as inflation climbs. Historical observations of the inverse correlation between unemployment and inflation led to the development of the Phillips curve expressing the relationship. For a time at least, higher inflation can spur demand while lowering inflation-adjusted labour costs, fueling job gains.

Eventually, though, the bill for persistently high inflation must come due in the form of a painful downturn that resets expectations, or else chronic economic underperformance.

8. Inflation Can Cause Painful Recessions

The trouble with the trade-off between inflation and unemployment is that prolonged acceptance of higher inflation to protect jobs may cause inflation expectations to rise to the point where they set off an inflationary spiral of price hikes and pay increases, as happened in the U.S. during the stagflation of the 1970s.

To regain lost credibility and convince everyone again it would control inflation, the Fed was subsequently forced to raise interest rates much higher and keep them high for a longer period of time. That, in turn, caused unemployment to soar, and to stay high for longer than would likely have been the case had the Fed not allowed inflation to spiral so high.

9. Inflation Hurts Bonds & Growth Stocks
Bonds are generally considered to be low-risk investments that provide regular interest income at a fixed rate. Inflation (especially high inflation) impairs the value of bonds by lowering the present value of that income.

As interest rates increase in response to rising or elevated inflation, so does the yield on newly issued bonds. The market price of bonds issued previously at a lower yield then drops proportionally, since bond prices are the inverse of bond yields. Investors with Treasury bonds are still in line for the expected coupon payments, followed by principal repayment at maturity. But those who sell their bonds before maturity will receive less as a result of the increased market yields.

There is less of a consensus about whether high inflation hurts or helps stocks overall. Conclusions depend on the definition of high inflation and whether the historical record cited includes the 1970s, a lost decade for U.S. stocks amid stagflation.

Growth stocks, which tend to be more expensive, are notoriously allergic to inflation. Inflation discounts the present value of their future cash flows more heavily, just as it does for high-duration bonds. Technology and consumer stocks have lagged during past episodes of high or rising inflation.

10. Inflation Boosts Real Estate, Energy, & Value Stocks
Real estate has historically served as a hedge against inflation since landlords can protect themselves by raising rents even as inflation erodes the real cost of fixed-rate mortgages.

Rising commodity prices can cause inflation to accelerate. Once it does, commodities can change when growth slows. This is particularly true of energy commodities that tend to continue to outperform.

Unsurprisingly, energy equities, real estate investment trusts (REITs), and value stocks have historically outperformed during episodes of high or rising inflation.

Areas Impacted:
Inflation can have a positive impact on the economy. As noted above, a little inflation can be a good thing for the economy. When prices rise at a moderate rate, people continue to spend rather than save their cash. Most consumers open up their wallets even when there's a slight increase in prices because they often expect things to get more expensive in the future.

But savers will take a hit as inflation continues to rise. For instance:

- You'll have to increase the amount of money you save for retirement. That's because the target amount you set to match your current lifestyle won't be enough when it comes time to leave the workforce. Put simply, you won't be able to afford to support yourself in retirement if you don't adjust how much you're saving based on inflation.
- The value of certain fixed-income investments drops. For example, the rate of return on government-issued securities drops as inflation increases. And when returns drop, more people may decide to sell them, which decreases their value.
- The value of the national debt rises because the amount of interest owed on that debt increases. When this happens, governments may be forced to raise taxes or cut down on spending.

One thing to keep in mind is that not every asset's value moves in the same direction because of inflation. So just because one rises, the other may drop. For instance, mortgage rates may rise but the value of your home may drop.

Chapter seven

Who Benefits and Who Doesn't?

As with any other economic phenomenon, inflation comes with both winners and losers. Let's take a look at who gains from inflation and who doesn't.

Who benefits;
Inflation can be a boon for certain borrowers. Consider mortgagors who have fixed-rate loans on their homes. If you have a rate locked in at 5% and inflation

causes interest rates to rise, you won't be affected. That can't be said about your neighbour who may have an ARM that changes based on market rates.

You're probably going to be in luck if you're in the market for a new home. That's because higher prices (and, therefore, higher interest rates) often knock out the competition, boosting the amount of inventory available. So if you can afford it, you're likely going to be able to get the pick of the lot.

Who It Doesn't

Since inflation reduces purchasing power, consumers represent the primary group who stand to lose when prices rise. That's because their money doesn't go nearly as far and allows them a limited number of goods and services they can purchase. Most consumers tend to think twice about buying a big-ticket item, such as a new appliance or a new car when inflation is high.

Home buyers may also feel the pinch during these times. That's because higher prices mean higher interest rates, which makes borrowing more expensive.

People who are on a fixed income are also negatively affected by inflation. Consider retirees who receive Social Security. Although they may receive COLA increases in their benefits, it may not be enough to sustain the same standard of living they're used to when prices increase to certain levels.

What Is Inflation's Primary Effect?

Inflation is the rise in prices of goods and services. It causes the purchasing power of a currency to decline, making a representative basket of goods and services increasingly more expensive.

How Can Inflation Benefit Homeowners?

Homeowners with fixed-rate mortgages benefit from inflation because it discounts the present value of their future mortgage payments. As housing prices rise as a result of inflation, home equity increases. Finally, homeowners who rent out their homes can increase rents with inflation.

What Is Deflation?

Deflation is a sustained period of broadly declining prices. Deflation is often the result of a severe economic contraction that causes consumers and businesses to curtail spending and investing. Deflation is destabilising because it makes it harder to service debts.

The Bottom Line
Inflation can be a blessing and a curse, depending on how you look at it. On the one hand, governments and central banks plan for manageable price increases by setting inflationary targets and consumers respond by spending as prices tend to increase at a nominal rate. But that changes when inflation overheats. It can diminish the purchasing power of consumers. When inflation runs rampant, governments generally raise interest rates, reduce the amount of money banks must have on reserve, and cut back on the money supply.

Six Ways to Fight Inflation
Personal Consumption Expenditure (PCE) inflation rose by 6.3 percent over the past year and 0.6 percent last month according to new data from the Bureau of Economic Analysis, well above the Federal Reserve's 2 percent annual (0.166 percent monthly) target. Consumer Price Index (CPI) inflation is up 8.6 percent – the highest in over four decades.

While it is mainly the responsibility of the Federal Reserve to fight inflation, smart fiscal policy can help assist the Fed in reducing the inflation rate while minimising negative effects on output, employment, and financial stability.

As President Biden has remarked numerous times, "bringing down the deficit is one way to ease inflationary pressures." This could include avoiding further deficit-boosting measures; lowering health care costs; raising tax revenue; reducing consumption-oriented spending; promoting work, savings, and investment; and/or lowering energy, trade, and procurement costs.
 As the Federal Reserve continues to raise interest rates and shrink its balance sheet in order to temper demand and reduce inflationary pressures, Congress and the President should use tools at their disposal to assist in the effort to fight inflation. They could reduce inflation in the following ways:

Personal Consumption Expenditure (PCE) inflation rose by 6.3 percent over the past year and 0.6 percent last month according to new data from the Bureau of Economic Analysis, well above the Federal Reserve's 2 percent annual (0.166

percent monthly) target. Consumer Price Index (CPI) inflation is up 8.6 percent – the highest in over four decades.

While it is mainly the responsibility of the Federal Reserve to fight inflation, smart fiscal policy can help assist the Fed in reducing the inflation rate while minimising negative effects on output, employment, and financial stability.

As President Biden has remarked numerous times, "bringing down the deficit is one way to ease inflationary pressures." This could include avoiding further deficit-boosting measures; lowering health care costs; raising tax revenue; reducing consumption-oriented spending; promoting work, savings, and investment; and/or lowering energy, trade, and procurement costs.

As the Federal Reserve continues to raise interest rates and shrink its balance sheet in order to temper demand and reduce inflationary pressures, Congress and the President should use tools at their disposal to assist in the effort to fight inflation. They could reduce inflation in the following ways:

- Stop Digging: At a minimum, Congress should avoid making the inflationary environment worse. They could do so by ending remaining COVID relief – including the student debt repayment pause and enhanced Medicaid payments to states – that are boosting price levels by 0.2 to 0.7 percentage points. They should also avoid adding more to the deficit, whether through a gas tax holiday, student debt cancellation, expanded veterans benefits, a "competitiveness" bill, aid to restaurants, retirement reforms, or new tax cuts.
- Lower Health Care Costs: The federal government directly influences many health care prices through payments to Medicare providers and Medicare Advantage plans as well as through its coverage of prescription drugs. Thoughtful health care reforms can reduce prices and the utilisation of care, which would ease inflationary pressures. Based on one study, each percentage point reduction in Medicare costs would reduce the inflation rate by 5 to 15 basis points.
- Reform the Tax Code to Raise More Revenue: The size and structure of the tax code affect inflation mainly through their impacts on the size and distribution of after-tax income. Tax increases can reduce demand in a

distributionally desirable way, putting downward pressure on inflation. Lawmakers can further reduce inflation by limiting tax expenditures and subsidies that drive up specific prices in the economy.

- Limit Discretionary Spending, Reduce Consumption-Oriented Spending, and Shrink Aid to States: To further temper demand, policymakers should limit the size of next year's appropriations, reimpose discretionary spending caps to limit future spending growth, and reduce spending on various programs ranging from farm subsidies to Social Security benefits for high earners. In light of the $900 billion of federal aid sent to cash-flush state and local governments, lawmakers could also consider reducing certain state and local funding.
- Promote Work, Savings, and Investment: Increased labour supply, capital supply, productivity, and personal savings can help to reduce inflationary pressures. Policymakers could reduce barriers to work, for example, by eliminating the Social Security earnings test, allowing older workers to collect the Earned Income Tax Credit, improving work requirements in some programs, providing vocational training for disabled workers, and other reforms. They could encourage savings by promoting the purchase of inflation-indexed bonds, expanding the saver's credit, or improving tax preferences for retirement savings. They could also support investments through regulatory reforms and targeted federal funding. Importantly, failing to offset new investments will undermine any inflationary gains, as higher demand would offset higher supply.
- Lower Energy, Trade, and Procurement Costs: Beyond the normal supply and demand channels, government policies and regulations can influence the before- or after-tax price of various goods and services. For example, the government can help control inflation by ensuring it is getting the best price for its dollars, reducing tariffs that push up the price of goods, ending regulations that boost shipping costs, and encouraging extraction of fossil fuels and production of renewable energy, among other means.

The Federal Reserve is rightly responsible for maintaining price stability and should continue to take steps to bring inflation down. However, navigating a "soft landing" – in which inflation is brought under control without triggering a recession – on its own will be challenging for the Fed, particularly if lawmakers continue to use fiscal policy to worsen inflationary pressures.

Congress and the President should instead work together to assist the Federal Reserve in fighting inflation, including by paying for new policies, ending COVID relief, lowering health care costs, raising revenue, reducing spending, boosting the supply side of the economy, and lowering prices within their purview.

Chapter Eight.

9 WAYS TO COMBAT THE IMPACT OF INFLATION9 WAYS TO COMBAT THE IMPACT OF INFLATION.

Throughout the past year, nearly everyone has felt the effects of record-breaking inflation. While dealing with higher grocery prices to steep energy costs, many people have wondered how to make their paychecks go further. Below are strategies to cope with inflation today, followed by ideas for preparing your finances to withstand inflation's effects in the future.

6 Ways to Cope with Inflation in the Short-Term.
 1. Monitor your budget. Pay special attention to bills on autopay. While autopay is a helpful feature to ensure you're not late on payments, it can also make it easy to stop paying attention. If that happens, you could miss price increases on subscriptions and services.

2. Identify which categories (food, gas, clothes, entertainment) have gone up the most and consider how you can lower them. For instance, the cost of gas has risen across the nation. Perhaps you can organise a carpool, ride bikes to nearby places, or strategically plan weekend errands to cut down on drive time.

3. Prioritise your spending and determine what you can eliminate or where you can cut back without too much pain. For families, especially, seemingly small expenses can add up fast. If you have several streaming channels, consider whether you can keep just a few of your favourites and cancel the others. If you enjoy trips to the coffee shop, try brewing your favourite drinks at home. Expensive gym memberships could be replaced with at-home workouts. Brand name groceries can be swapped for generic items.

4. Shop wisely. If you need to shop for household items or clothing, look for quality second-hand items in good condition before splurging on brand-new, price-inflated options. While you're at it, look around your own home to see if you have any unused items to sell while there might be a bigger market for pre-owned goods. When making a larger purchase, prioritise durability to save yourself from costly repairs or replacements down the road.

5. Reduce your energy usage. Energy costs are closely tied to inflation, so do an energy audit of your home and vehicles. Fix draughty windows and doors, use energy-efficient light bulbs, unplug electronics when you're not using them, keep your thermostat at a reasonable temperature (and schedule more efficient temperatures when your family typically isn't home), and inflate your car tires for maximum fuel efficiency.

6.For many people, annual reviews are approaching at work. Prepare to ask for a raise by quantifying your contributions and sharing stories of your positive impacts. Also, be ready with inflation numbers to ensure your raise can at least keep up with the cost of living.

3 Ways to Prepare for Inflation Long-Term

1. Try to add more money to your emergency fund. As expenses go up, so will the amount of financial cushion you'll need to cover unexpected costs or your expenses between jobs. So reevaluate the right amount and squirrel away any extra money you can until you meet your new savings goal.

2. Cut down any debt that comes with variable interest rates. As inflation continues to rise, those rates could increase. Consider refinancing to a fixed-rate loan. If that's not possible, you may want to prioritise paying down loans with variable rates.

3. Keep up with inflation by looking for ways to grow your money over time. If you can create some extra funds now through smart spending, then it may be a good time to start investing. Stocks often stay ahead of inflation over time. But if you don't have enough extra income to invest, consider moving any cash that you don't need for near-term expenses from a low-interest checking account to one that has a higher interest

yield like a Certificates of Deposit (CD), a money market account, or a high-yield savings account which can often be linked to your checking account to protect you from overdrafts.

How Fiscal Restraint Can Help Fight Inflation

Government support was vital to help people and firms survive pandemic lockdowns and support the economic recovery.

But where inflation is high and persistent, across-the-board fiscal support is not warranted. Most governments have already dialled back pandemic support, as noted in our October Fiscal Monitor.

With many people still struggling, governments should continue to prioritise helping the most vulnerable to cope with soaring food and energy bills and cover other costs—but governments should also avoid adding to aggregate demand that risks dialling up inflation. In many advanced and emerging economies, fiscal restraint can lower inflation while reducing debt.

Fiscal consolidation, limiting debt

Central banks are raising interest rates to dampen demand and contain inflation, which in many countries is at its highest levels since the 1980s. Because rapid price gains are costly to society and detrimental to stable economic growth, monetary policy must act decisively.

While monetary policy has the tools to subdue inflation, fiscal policy can put the economy on a sounder long-term footing through investment in infrastructure, health care, and education; fair distribution of incomes and opportunities through an equitable tax and transfer system; and provision of basic public services. The overall fiscal balance, however, affects the demand for goods and services, and inflationary pressures.

A smaller deficit cools aggregate demand and inflation, so the central bank doesn't need to raise rates as much. Moreover, with global financial conditions constraining budgets, and public debt ratios above pre-pandemic levels, reducing deficits also addresses debt vulnerabilities.

Conversely, fiscal stimulus in the current high inflation environment would force central banks to slam on the brakes harder to curb inflation. Amid elevated public and private sector debt, this may raise risks for the financial system, as our Global Financial Stability Report described in October.

Demonstrating alignment

Against that backdrop, policymakers have a responsibility to provide strong protections to those in need, while paring back elsewhere or raising additional revenues to reduce the overall deficit. Fiscal responsibility—or even consolidation where needed—demonstrates that policymakers are aligned against inflation.

When fiscal adjustment is sustained, ideally through a medium-term fiscal framework that sketches the direction of policy over the next few years, it also addresses looming pressures on debt sustainability. These include ageing populations in most advanced and several emerging economies, and the need to rebuild buffers that can be deployed in future crises or economic downturns.

had become entrenched at high levels, and fiscal policy was expansionary. The Fed had to raise rates sharply to rein in inflation, causing a collapse in housing investment and historically large appreciation of the dollar. Manufacturing was hard hit, leading to calls for trade protectionism.

That historical episode is relevant for many countries facing similar challenges today. A more balanced removal of policy stimulus, including fiscal restraint, can reduce the risk that some parts of the economy—especially those most sensitive to interest rates—experience disproportionate effects, or that large swings in the currency heighten trade tensions.

This would also reduce risk globally. Less abrupt interest rate hikes would imply a more gradual tightening of financial conditions and mitigate financial stability risks. This would tend to limit adverse spillovers to emerging market economies and reduce the risk of sovereign debt distress. Avoiding a sharp appreciation of the US dollar or other major currencies would also lessen pressures on emerging markets that borrow in those currencies.

While many central banks are tightening policy in response to the large and persistent rise in global inflation, the policy mix matters. Fiscal restraint will reduce the cost of bringing inflation back to target in a timely way, compared with the alternative of leaving monetary policy alone to act.

Fiscal Policy Can Help Tame Inflation and Protect the Most Vulnerable.
High inflation can impose serious and lasting costs on the economy and people. But the distributive effects of inflation—the way it transfers money from some individuals to others—are complex.

To respond effectively to the sharpest upsurge in inflation in three decades and to address the damage done to households, policymakers should have a better understanding of how inflation affects various segments of society in different places.

In our April 2023 Fiscal Monitor, we study the effects of (unexpected) inflation on people's well-being from mid-2021 to mid-2022—a period when food and energy prices rose earlier and faster than other prices. The chapter offers several lessons for policymakers on the impact of inflation on households' budgets and how fiscal policy can help curb inflation while supporting the vulnerable.

Impact on public finances:
Analysing how inflation affects public finances, our main finding is that unexpected inflation—such as in the recent episode—erodes the real value of government debt at the expense of bondholders. For countries with debt exceeding 50 percent of GDP, each percentage point of unexpected ("surprise") increase in inflation reduces public debt by 0.6 percentage points of GDP, with the effect lasting for several years.
As inflation becomes persistent and better anticipated, however, it stops contributing to declining debt ratios.

Likewise, deficit-to-GDP ratios initially decline as spending fails to keep pace with the rise in the monetary value of the economy's output. But such effects fade even quicker.

Impact on households:

Based on public surveys of thousands of households in six economies (Colombia, Finland, France, Kenya, Mexico, and Senegal), we find that inflation from mid-2021 to mid-2022 impacted people through three main channels: their consumption patterns; their income from wages, pensions, or transfers; and their assets and liabilities. The below chart displays the estimated effects of these channels to a developing economy (Kenya) and to an advanced economy (France), prior to any new government intervention in support of households.

Although the impact varies across countries (and across income groups), the surveys reveal that:

- The faster rise in food prices compared to other prices hurt poor families disproportionately because food represents a higher share of their total consumption. This effect was most pronounced in low-income countries.

- Inflation eroded real incomes in commodity-importing countries, as wages across all income groups did not keep pace with prices.

- As inflation eroded the monetary value of assets and liabilities, families with negative net worth benefitted at the expense of creditors, particularly in countries with developed financial and credit markets.

- Redistributive wealth effects of inflation were also influenced by the age of the head of household: young families, which tend to be net borrowers, experienced gains through the wealth channels, whereas old households saw their wealth eroded.

Curbing inflation while protecting the vulnerable.
Fiscal policy can support monetary policy in dealing with inflation because it also affects aggregate demand. Our statistical evidence suggests that fiscal policy's impact on inflation has changed over the decades. For advanced economies we find that, since 1985, reducing public expenditure by 1 percentage point of GDP lowers inflation by half a percentage point.

In addition, fiscal policy can also help protect the vulnerable.
Curbing inflation while protecting the vulnerable

Fiscal policy can support monetary policy in dealing with inflation because it also affects aggregate demand. Our statistical evidence suggests that fiscal policy's impact on inflation has changed over the decades. For advanced economies we find that, since 1985, reducing public expenditure by 1 percentage point of GDP lowers inflation by half a percentage point. In addition, fiscal policy can also help protect the vulnerable.

Curbing inflation while protecting the vulnerable

Fiscal policy can support monetary policy in dealing with inflation because it also affects aggregate demand. Our statistical evidence suggests that fiscal policy's impact on inflation has changed over the decades. For advanced economies we find that, since 1985, reducing public expenditure by 1 percentage point of GDP lowers inflation by half a percentage point.